JEWEL of the MALL

WORLD WAR II MEMORIAL

Photographs by Stephen R. Brown • Introduction by Senator Robert Dole

Dedicated to Edward and Joan Brown

The Greatest of the "Great Generation"

JEWEL OF THE MALL: THE WORLD WAR II MEMORIAL

ISBN 978-0-9766150-3-3

© Stephen R. Brown 2011

202-667-1965

srb@srbphoto.com

www.wwiimemorialbook.com • www.jewelofthemall.com

Photographs Copyright Stephen R. Brown 2003-2011 • www.stephenbrownstudio.com

Sculpture Copyright Raymond Kaskey 2002 • www.kaskeystudio.com

Table of Contents

Introduction

by Senator Robert Dole

In May of 2004, I joined thousands of fellow World War II veterans assembled on the Mall to dedicate another war memorial. Actually, that's not quite right. We don't build memorials to war—we build memorials to those who fight wars, to the millions who wear their country's uniform, to the even greater numbers on the home front who support them with their labor and their love, and to the precious freedom we fight to preserve.

We build memorials to offer instruction as well as inspiration. The lessons they teach are as relevant at Khe San and Khandahar as at Bataan, Gettysburg, or Valley Forge. Beginning with the most important lesson of war: trust your comrades as if your life depends on it, because it usually does. That's not all you learn on the battlefield. You learn that the blood spilled in conflict is all the same color, whether it comes from the sons of immigrants or the grandsons of slaves.

In a dangerous world, these are lessons that each generation must learn for itself. In the early years of the 20th century, my father fibbed about his age in the hope that he might go "Over There." In the wake of Pearl Harbor I joined the Army, and actually got "Over There." It was the children of the so-called Greatest Generation who went to Vietnam. They proved themselves every bit as great in their fidelity to freedom; even greater, in a sense. Those who fought in Vietnam risked every bit as much as the men of D-Day and Guadalcanal and did so without the political or popular support that we enjoyed.

In the words of Dwight D. Eisenhower, "I hate war as only a soldier who has lived it can, only as one who has seen its brutality and stupidity." On the one hand, war represents the ultimate failure of mankind. Yet it also summons the greatest qualities of which human beings are capable: courage beyond measure, loyalty beyond words, sacrifice and ingenuity, and endurance beyond imagining.

In the end, it is their sacrifice, their service and their blood that sanctify the Mall. They are forever remembered here, in the company of Washington, Jefferson, Lincoln, and Roosevelt. May this be a source of consolation and pride to the families who love them, the comrades who mourn them, and the vast numbers who draw inspiration from their example; may God watch over this proud company; and may God bless the United States of America.

Bob Dole

Jewel of the Mall

by Stephen R. Brown

This book is dedicated to the "Greatest Generation" best exemplified by Senator Robert Dole. If he had not led the charge, I doubt the Memorial would have been finished or financed. Originally entitled "American Memory, American Vision," this book is also a tribute to the workers and artisans who completed this project in a mere two years. Their excitement was contagious. Their enthusiasm and ingenuity harkened back to the World War II effort on the Home Front. They made the impossible, possible.

My wonderful wife June and daughter Caitlin were supportive and enthusiastic throughout the project. Ray and Sherry Kaskey, Friedrich St.Florian, APEX Piping Systems, Laran Foundry, and construction superintendents David Tweedie and Barry Owenby made sure I had access to the site and cranes for photography. Joyce McCluney, Senator Dole's "right hand," kept my spirits high when funds were low. Mike Marshall of Senator Dole's office supervised my writing efforts.

In June 2003, I noticed construction on the World War II Memorial was finally underway. I called sculptor Ray Kaskey to congratulate him and kidded him about his aversion to press and photography. He said: "No problem... there's been no press whatever."

After all the planning by major architectural and construction firms, historical and fine art committees, no one had thought about thoroughly documenting this historic project. And while this project had no end of financial and bureaucratic difficulties, its historic and emotional appeal made it incumbent that I finish the book.

In 2002, I first photographed the casting and manufacturing of the 80,000 pound bronze eagle sculptures at the Laran Foundry in Pennsylvania. In September 2003, APEX Piping Systems, which had designed the internal structure and columns for the eagles, did a "trial" installation inside the foundry. Because they needed several cranes to

arrange the 80,000-pound sculptures, I set up large studio lights as far away from the action as possible and worked unobtrusively and carefully. In October and November, the eagles were shipped to Washington, and I was invited to document the installation of the eagles on the Mall.

It took three weeks to install the eight eagles and weld the laurel wreaths between them. I brought my safety harness and was given access to the cranes when the eagles were lifted into the air and lowered into place inside the Memorial Pavilions. During that period, veterans and their families came to watch the installation of the eagles. Even the cranes had eagles painted on them. It was thrilling!

This book is both a portfolio of the finished Memorial and a historical documentation of the construction in granite and bronze. As the eagles were lifted in the air against the DC skyline, they seemed absolutely enormous. Now, they seem "right-sized."

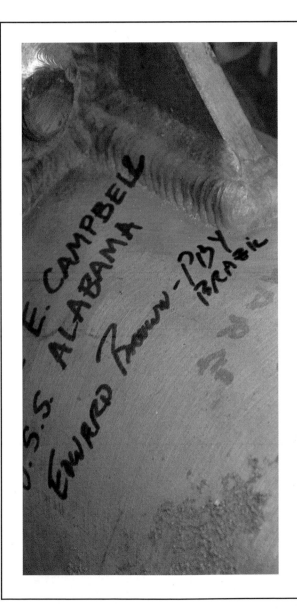

As you wander the site in the late evening, you can experience the genius of Ray Kaskey's high-flying eagles, wreaths, rope, and stars that adorn architect Friedrich St. Florian's majestic design. As you look out through the columns representing the states and territories that fought in World War II, they frame the other monuments on the Mall.

This Memorial is truly a masterpiece of artistic, architectural, and historical design, which I have come to see as the "Jewel of the Mall." Its classical design, intricate bronze work, fountains, and seating arrangements invite the visitor to rest and contemplate the price of freedom.

My biggest thrill, however, was the opportunity to write my father's name next to the names of many other veterans on the inner structure of the Southeast Atlantic Eagle (shown here on the right). He served in a PBY airplane—a submarine hunter—off the Coast of Brazil. He loved a difficult project and would have been delighted to see this beautiful memorial completed.

Since the book was published, I have had the opportunity to spend a few hours every week with Senator Dole at the Memorial as he greets WWII veterans. His dedication to his "band of brothers" is deep as is the love of the families who escort their fathers and grandfathers to this Memorial.

Stephen R. Brown

The Memorial

The World War II Memorial unifies the Mall joining the Washington Monument and Lincoln Memorial. Entering from 17th Street, you are greeted by twenty-four bas relief panels depicting scenes from the Atlantic Front on the North side and the Pacific Front on the South side. Other bas relief panels depict pivotal stages in the War and on the Home Front. The 7.4 acre Memorial surrounds the refurbished Rainbow Pool. Two granite pavilions enclose massive eagle sculptures by Raymond Kaskey. At the western end, there is a wall of 4048 stars, one commemorating every hundred Americans who died in World War II. The fifty-six columns adorned with oak and wheat wreaths made of bronze represent the contribution of the states and territories towards the war effort. The pillars are joined by a bronze sculpted rope symbolizing the bonding of a nation. The Memorial was designed by Friedrich St. Florian.

THEY HAVE GIVEN THEIR
SONS TO THE MILITARY
SERVICES. THEY HAVE
STOKED THE FURNACES
AND HURRIED THE
FACTORY WHEELS. THEY
HAVE MADE THE PLANES
AND WELDED THE TANKS,
RIVETED THE SHIPS AND
ROLLED THE SHELLS.

PRESIDENT FRANKLIN D. ROOSEVELT

OUR DEBT TO THE
HEROIC MEN AND VALIANT
WOMEN IN THE SERVICE
OF OUR COUNTRY CAN
NEVER BE REPAID. THEY
HAVE EARNED OUR
UNDYING GRATITUDE.
AMERICA WILL NEVER
FORGET THEIR SACRIFICES.

PRESIDENT HARRY S TRUMAN

Fountains

During the opening process, the fountains were tuned and re-tuned with computers and audio equipment to monitor the sound and flow of the fountains. Granite blocks were added to the centers of the waterfall fountains (Page 26) adjacent to the Wall of Stars, to distinguish the sound from the main fountains in the center of the plaza.

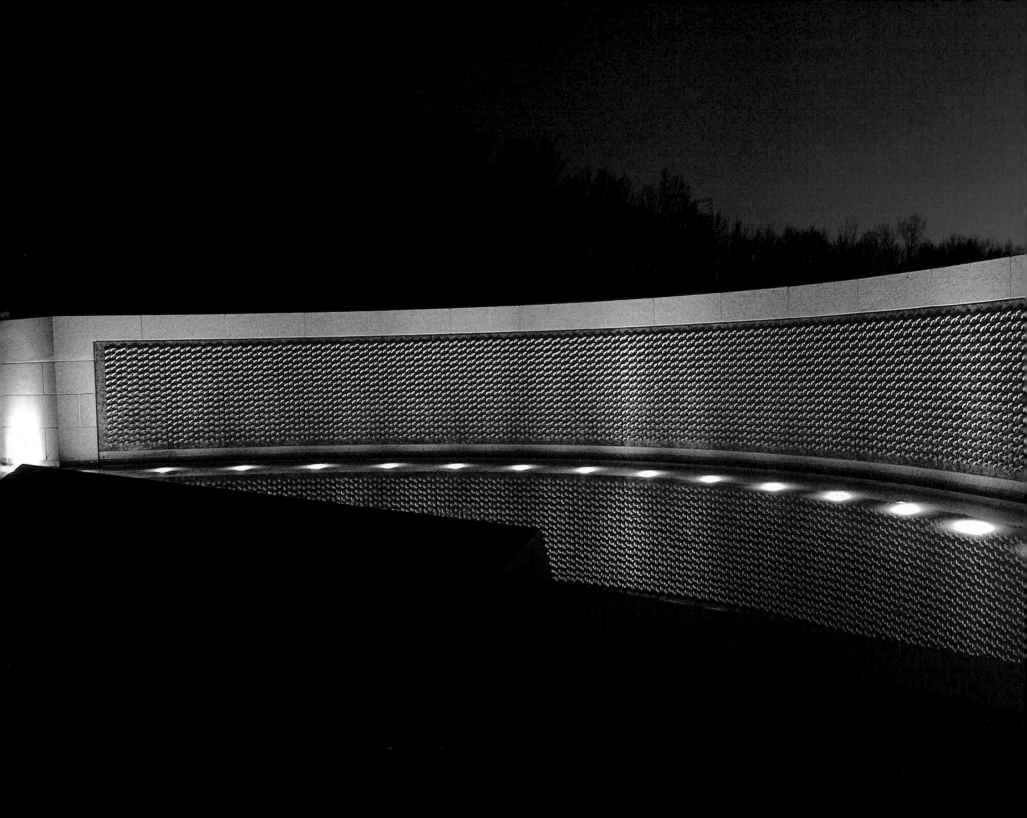

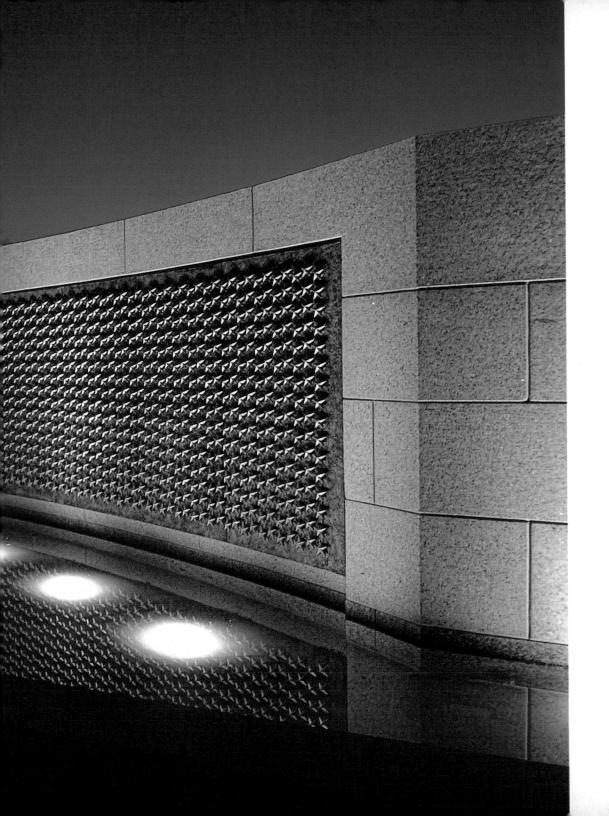

Wall of Stars

Each of the 4048 gold stars represents 100 Americans who died during the war. There is a computerized database of names of WWII Veterans who served. You can add any veterans you know along with a picture. The database is available through the Memorial's website.

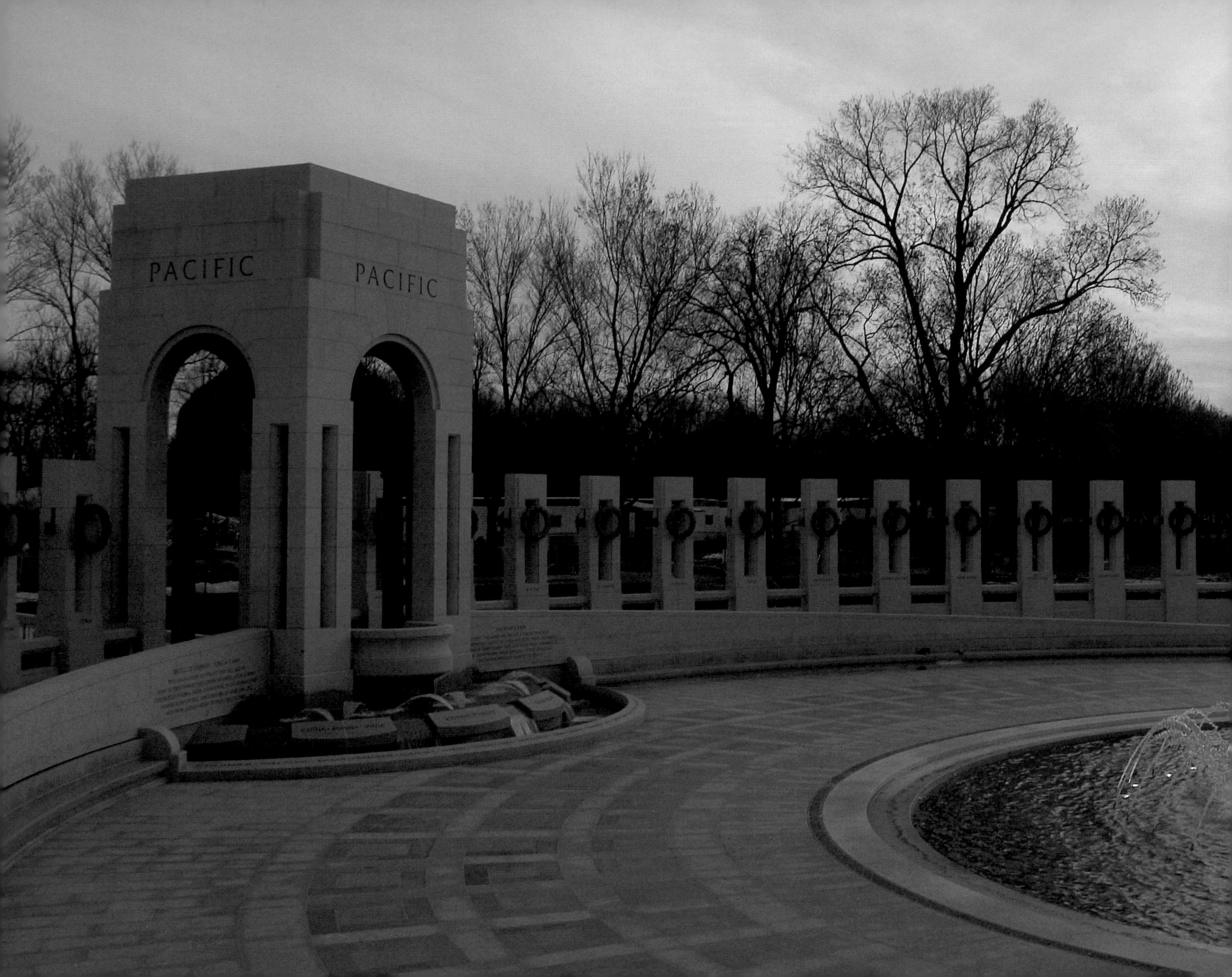
PACIFIC
PACIFIC

Grand Views

The unobstructed view of the Lincoln, Washington, and Jefferson Memorials was the product of democracy in action. The original plans for the Memorial called for thirty-six foot high columns. These were reduced to sixteen feet leaving the views intact. The original Rainbow Pool was taken out and restored to eighty percent of its original size in keeping with L'Enfant's original design for the Mall.

, 1942
DID, AND IN
AR...EVEN AGAINST
IN THE HUMAN SPIRIT–
LOR–THAT CAN LIFT
REDIBLE VICTORY
TODAY THE GUNS A
HAS ENDED. A GREAT VIC
NO LONGER RAIN DEATH–TH
MEN EVERYWHERE WALK U
THE ENTIRE WORLD IS
CHINA • BURMA • INDIA
SOUTHWEST PACIFIC
CENTRAL PACIFIC
NORTH PACIFIC
ORAL SEA • MIDWAY • GUADALCANAL • NEW GUINEA
TARAWA • KWAJALEIN • ATTU • SAIPAN TINIAN GUAM • PHILIPPIN

PACIFIC

THE WAR'S END
TODAY THE GUNS ARE SILENT. A GREAT
HAS ENDED. A GREAT VICTORY HAS BEEN
NO LONGER RAIN DEATH – THE SEAS BEAR
MEN EVERYWHERE WALK UPRIGHT IN
THE ENTIRE WORLD IS QUIETLY

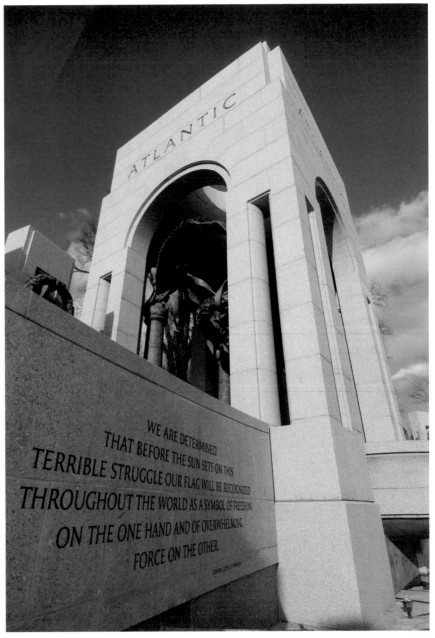

ATLANTIC

WE ARE DETERMINED
THAT BEFORE THE SUN SETS ON THIS
TERRIBLE STRUGGLE OUR FLAG WILL BE RECOGNIZED
THROUGHOUT THE WORLD AS A SYMBOL OF FREEDOM
ON THE ONE HAND AND OF OVERWHELMING
FORCE ON THE OTHER.

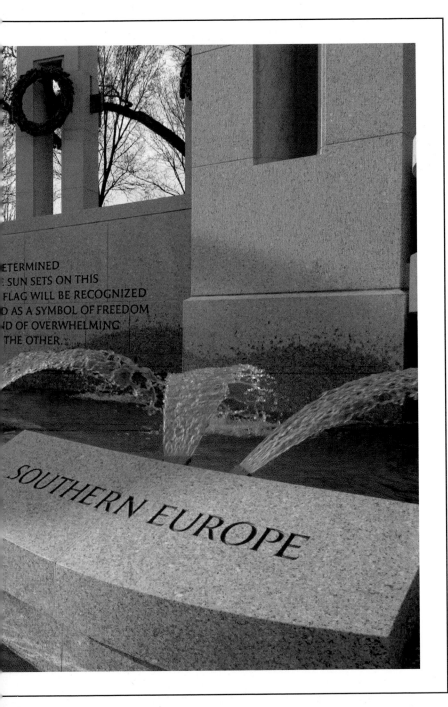

...ETERMINED
...E SUN SETS ON THIS
...FLAG WILL BE RECOGNIZED
...D AS A SYMBOL OF FREEDOM
...ND OF OVERWHELMING
...THE OTHER...

SOUTHERN EUROPE

BATTLE OF MIDWAY   JUNE 4-7,
THEY HAD NO RIGHT TO WIN. YET THEY DIL
DOING SO THEY CHANGED THE COURSE OF A WAR
THE GREATEST OF ODDS, THERE IS SOMETHING IN TI
A MAGIC BLEND OF SKILL, FAITH AND VALOR-TI
MEN FROM CERTAIN DEFEAT TO INCREDIBLE

Middle of the Mall

In the short time it has been open, the World War II Memorial has become Washington's most popular location with approximately fifteen to twenty million visitors each year. The main plaza is set down in the site so that the view of the surrounding monuments and memorials is framed by the columns and sculpture. On the next page, a view taken just weeks before the Memorial was opened shows the Western vista from a crane. You can see that the bas reliefs had not been installed.

Making a Memorial

This October 2003 view of the construction site was particularly unnerving as the Memorial had to be finished by May 25, 2004, a mere seven months away. Several trailers behind the Memorial were filled with computer generated construction plans used to fit the quarried stone together. Below the level here are enormous pump rooms used to power the fountains.

Guiding Lights

Key Figures in Shaping the Memorial

BG (ret.) Pat Foote, USA; Ambassador F. Haydn Williams, Jan Evans Houser, and Rolly Kidder helped found *Friends of the National WWII Memorial*. With **NPS Superintendent Peggy O'Dell,** they laid wreaths at the WWII Memorial on Veterans Day 2008. *Friends* mission is to educate the public to the great significance of World War II in the 20th Century and conduct band and ceremonial events during the year.

Architect Friedrich St. Florian, based in Providence, R.I., was selected to design the memorial through an open, national competition in 1996. He is now Dean Emeritus of the Rhode Island School of Design.

Stanley Wojtusik, 78, a Veteran of the Battle of the Bulge. His moving testimony in front of Congress inspired the passage of the long-overdue Memorial legislation.

BEFORE: A view of the original reflecting pool with the Lincoln in the background. The newly renovated reflecting pool is eighty percent of the size of the original and mirrors and enhances the WWII Memorial.

AFTER: This photograph shows what the view of the Lincoln Memorial looks like now, with the World War II Memorial surrounding the Rainbow Pool.

Making a Memorial

Sculpture

Ray Kaskey (right), sculptor for the World War II Memorial, oversaw the largest bronze project in contemporary history. In five years, his studio produced four bronze columns, eight bronze eagles, two bronze laurel wreaths for the archways, twenty-four bronze bas reliefs for the ceremonial entrance, four thousand and forty-eight sculpted gold stars for the Freedom Wall, one hundred and twelve bronze wreaths with armatures, fifty-two bronze ropes for the pillars, and the two flagpoles which mark the entrance to the Memorial.

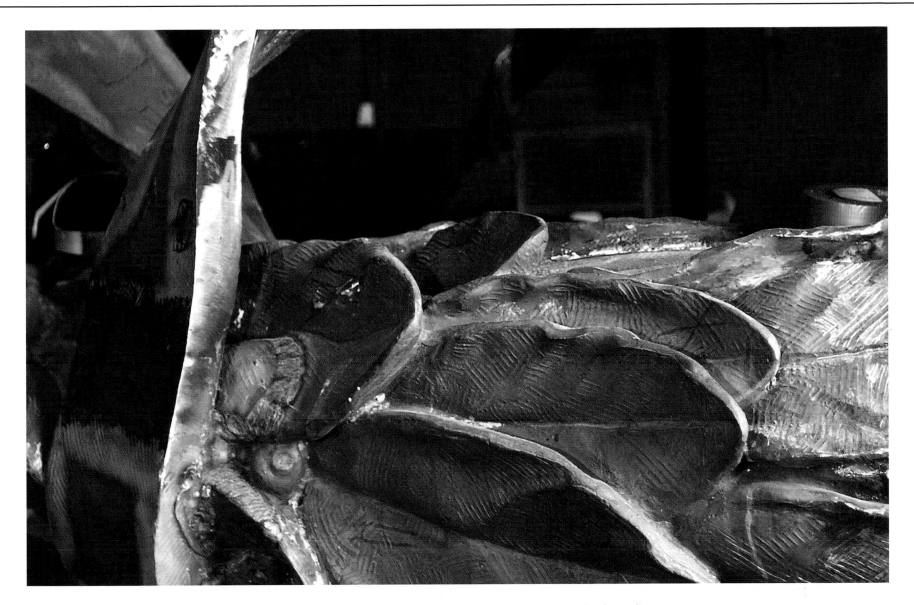

Ray Kaskey inspects the $1/2$" x 6" piece of stainless steel which surrounds and supports the laurel wreath. It is the structural triumph behind the suspension of the laurel wreath. The steel was cold rolled in a continuous piece and the butt ends of the steel welded to the eagle's beak.

Making a Memorial

Trial Installation

APEX Piping Workers weld and bolt the eagles together during trial installations of the two sets of four twelve-foot high eagles (on eighteen-foot bases) for a total weight of approximately 80,000 pounds. Three of the eagles (right) stand awaiting the fourth eagle and laurel wreath to be lifted by crane and put in place. The 5000-pound laurel wreath was suspended from the beaks of the eagles. On location, an X-ray machine was used to inspect the final welds. The bronze skin was treated with chemicals to give it a uniform color.

Making a Memorial

Monumental Drama

After delivery to the site, the eagles were lifted across the plaza and **Patrick Oakes and Scott Craig** of APEX Piping Systems (Pages 68-69)—builders of the interior skeleton and columns for the eagles—guide the padded eagle into the South Pavilion. The eight 20,000 pound eagles and laurel wreaths were transported to the Mall and very carefully lifted into place using two cranes. The tension during this part of the installation was extraordinarily high. As they were lowered into place, the eagles cleared the pavilion opening with three inches to spare.

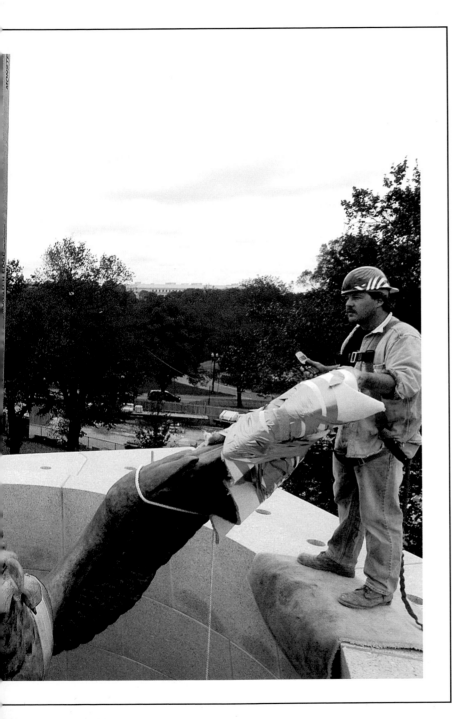

Making a Memorial

Granite

Granite was chosen for its aesthetic appeal, superior strength, durability, and water resistance. The two principal stones selected for the memorial are "Kershaw" for the vertical elements and "Green County" for the main plaza paving stone. "Kershaw" is quarried in South Carolina, while "Green County" is quarried in Georgia. Two green stones—"Rio Verde" and "Moss Green"—were used for accent paving on the plaza. Both are quarried in Brazil.

"Academy Black" and "Mount Airy" were used to reconstruct the Rainbow Pool. "Mount Airy," quarried in North Carolina, is the original coping stone of the Rainbow Pool. An apron of "Academy Black," quarried in California, was used for the vertical interior spaces.

Making a Memorial

Stone Carvers

John and Nick Benson of Rhode Island carved the quotations into the granite. They created a unique typeface for the World War II Memorial. The Bensons operate the oldest family-run business in the U.S. They designed and carved the type in stone for the Iwo Jima Memorial, the Kennedy Memorial in Washington, D.C., and the Civil Rights Memorial in Alabama.

PEARL HARBOR
DECEMBER 7, 1941, A DATE
WHICH WILL LIVE IN INFAMY...
NO MATTER HOW LONG IT
MAY TAKE US TO OVERCOME
HIS PREMEDITATED INVASIO
THE AMERICAN PEOPLE, I
THEIR RIGHTEOUS MIGHT
WILL WIN THROUGH
TO ABSOLUTE VICTORY.

PRESIDENT FRANKLIN D. ROOS

Joe Moss (left), a Master Stone Carver worked with the Bensons on this project, along with **Christine DeMarco (above)**, an apprentice carver from Rhode Island. She is staining the type with a lithochrome lacquer to highlight the letters. There are 3875 letters in the Memorial, all carved by hand.

Making a Memorial

Populating the Bas Reliefs

Sculptor Raymond Kaskey works (Pages 80-81) with World War II re-enactors, **Roland Blue and Brooks Tegler,** in period uniforms. Kaskey poses them on a roundtable to prepare photographs from a variety of perspectives. The photos served as guides for the three dimensional creation of the bas reliefs. His assistants, **Joanna Blake (Page 83), Perry Carsley (right), and Aaron Sykes** model the figures out of clay using the photographs for reference. Each of the bas reliefs contains a minimum of eight figures and took approximately one hundred hours to sculpt. The drawings were reviewed for historical accuracy and aesthetic appeal before any work could commence.

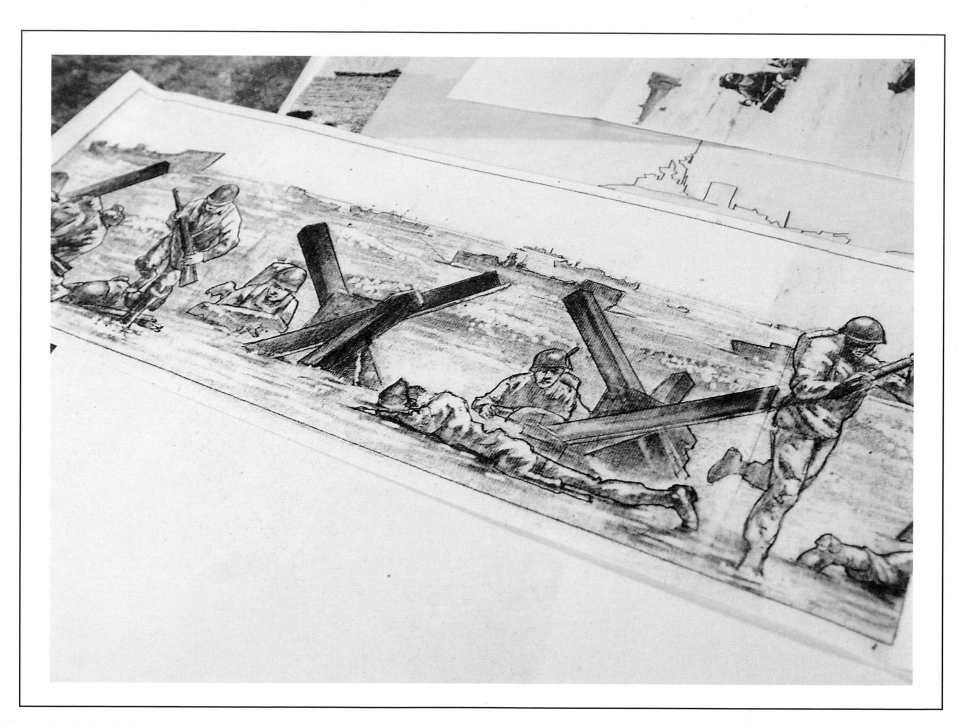

Making a Memorial

The Lost Wax Process

The clay models for the bas reliefs were shipped to the **Laran Foundry** in Pennsylvania where the rubber molds (Page 86) were made. These molds were then used to create wax positives of each panel (Page 87). The wax positives are used to make a negative mold into which the bronze was poured. When casting, bronze expands and contracts so the final measurements were a great source of concern as the granite walls and frames (Pages 48-49) of the Memorial were already in place. Selected bas reliefs can be seen in place on pages 90-91.

First Step (left): A rubber compound is poured over the clay models and left to harden. This creates a mold that is the exact negative of the original model.

Second Step. A wax positive is created in the mold. A plumbing system is created so the wax can be melted out and the bronze can fill the mold. Hence the name "Lost Wax Process."

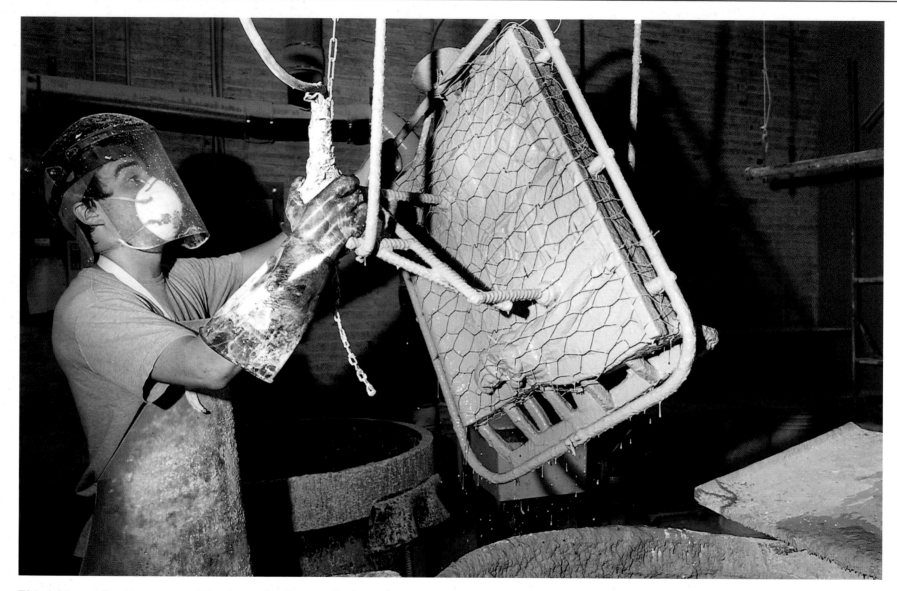

Third Step: After the wax positive is made, the wax is then dipped into a sand-like ceramic slurry. After this dries and hardens, the wax is burned out and the bronze is poured into the negative mold.

Fourth Step (right): Once the ceramic molds have been broken off the final bronze sculpture, the pieces are welded together and burnished until the sculptor is satisfied with their look.

PACIFIC

More information on the twenty-four bas reliefs is available through Kaskey Studio, Inc.

A Living Memorial

I have had the privilege of watching this seven acres of granite and bronze come to life. World War II Veterans and their families visit the Memorial regularly, and it is the most popular site on the Mall today. Honor Flight (see founders Jeff Miller and Earl Morse on Page 96) flies veterans for free to see their Memorial. And Senators Robert and Elizabeth Dole are always there to greet them. It is one of the amazing charitable movements of our time. Families, towns, and veterans groups gathered together to raise millions to fly these WWII Veterans for free. These pages show the Memorial on a daily basis crowded with both young and old celebrating the lives of the greatest generation and in some cases just relaxing in the sun by a fountain. Tom Hanks, Steven Spielberg, Colin Powell, and many more have greeted vets and celebrated their service at the Memorial.

Earl Morse and Jeff Miller co-founded Honor Flight, a non-profit organization which flies veterans to Washington, D.C. to see the Memorial. The flights have been staffed by thousands of volunteers like **Jim McLaughlin and Mary Pettinato** who have "retired" and worked tirelessly to bring World War II Veterans to their Memorial. **Senator Dole** has personally welcomed most of them.

Ceremonies for veterans are often accompanied by festivities including buglers and bagpipers who lead the vets down into the ceremonial plaza. **Tom Hanks and Steven Spielberg** flew four hundred World War II veterans to Washington for a ceremony to celebrate their TV series "The Pacific."

Band of Brothers: They sometimes wear their old uniforms and bring memorabilia of fallen comrades. Organizations like Honor Flight bring in hundreds of veterans a year and stage elaborate ceremonies (right) at the memorial. When the Veterans return home, they are normally treated to a long-overdue homecoming. Ceremonies like these are repeated daily as the Honor Flights pay tribute.

THE WAR'S END

TODAY THE GUNS ARE SILENT. A GREAT TRAGEDY
...NDED. A GREAT VICTORY HAS BEEN WON. THE SKIES
...AIN DEATH-TH...
...ERE... ...MMERCE-

U.S. NAVAL

...7 Sept. 1942
... Mar. 1943
... Oct. 1943
...1 Nov 1943
...n 21 July 1944
...harged 9 Oct 1945

CONSTRUCTION BATTALION

William F. Stevenson
February 13, 1918
December 15, 2007

ENGINEERING DEPARTMENT

Memorial Overview

The Memorial honors the sixteen million who served in the U.S. armed forces during World War II, the more than 400,000 who died, and the millions who supported the war effort from home. Symbolic of this defining event of the 20th Century, the Memorial is a monument to the spirit, sacrifice, and commitment of the American people to the common defense of the nation and to the broader causes of peace and freedom from tyranny throughout the world. Above all, the Memorial stands as a symbol of American national unity, a timeless reminder of the moral strength and awesome power of a free people united and bonded together in a common and just cause.

HERE IN THE PRESENCE OF WASHINGTON AND LINCOLN,
THE EIGHTEENTH CENTURY FATHER AND THE OTHER
THE NINETEENTH CENTURY PRESERVER OF OUR NATION,
HONOR THOSE TWENTIETH CENTURY AMERICANS WHO
K UP THE STRUGGLE DURING THE SECOND WORLD
R AND MADE THE SACRIFICES TO PERPETUATE
E GIFT OUR FOREFATHERS ENTRUSTED TO US:
A NATION CONCEIVED IN LIBERTY AND JUSTICE.

AUTHORIZATION: President Clinton signed Public Law 103–32 on May 25, 1993, authorizing the *American Battle Monuments Commission* to establish a WWII Memorial in Washington, D.C, or its environs. It is the first national memorial dedicated to all who served during World War II and acknowledging the commitment and achievement of the entire nation.

SITE: The first step in establishing the WWII Memorial was the selection of an appropriate site. Congress provided legislative authority for siting the Memorial in the prime area of the nation's capital that includes the National Mall. The *National Park Service,* the *National Capital Planning Commission*, and the *Commission of Fine Arts* approved selection of the Rainbow Pool site at the east end of the Reflecting Pool between the Lincoln Memorial and the Washington Monument. President Clinton dedicated the memorial site during a ceremony on Veterans Day 1995.

DESIGN: Friedrich St. Florian, an architect based in Providence, R.I., was selected to design the Memorial through an open, national competition in 1996. **Leo A. Daly**, an international architecture firm, assembled the winning team with St. Florian as the design architect. The team also included associate design architect **George E. Hartman** of Hartman-Cox Architects, landscape architect **James van Sweden** of Oehme van Sweden & Associates, sculptor **Ray Kaskey**, and stone carver **Nick Benson**. St. Florian's design concept was approved by the *National Park Service*, the *Commission of Fine Arts* and the *National Capital Planning Commission* in 1998. The three agencies approved the preliminary design in 1999, the final architectural design and ancillary elements in 2000, granite selections in 2001, and sculpture and inscriptions in 2002 and 2003.

FUND-RAISING: The memorial was funded primarily by private contributions. **Former Senator Bob Dole** and Federal Express Corporation founder and CEO **Frederick W. Smith** led the fund raising campaign. The memorial campaign received more than $197 million in cash and pledges, only $16 million of which was provided by the federal government.

CONSTRUCTION: The Memorial was built by the joint venture of **Tompkins Builders/ Grunley-Walsh Construction**. *The General Services Administration* provided project management and contracting services to support the establishment and construction of the Memorial and the **Gilbane Building Company** provided construction quality management services for the project. Construction began in September 2001 and the Memorial was opened to the public in April 2004.

DEDICATION: The four-day dedication celebration was held Memorial Day weekend, from May 27–30, 2004. The official dedication ceremony was Saturday, May 29, 2004. *The American Battle Monuments Commission* is an independent, executive branch agency with 11 commissioners and a secretary appointed by the President. The ABMC administers, operates and maintains 25 permanent U.S. military cemeteries and 25 memorial structures in 15 countries around the world, including three memorials in the United States. The commission is also responsible for the establishment of other memorials in the U.S. as directed by Congress.

WORLD WAR II MEMORIAL DESIGN: The World War II Memorial design recognizes that the site itself pays special tribute to America's WWII generation. The memorial design creates a special place within the vast openness of the National Mall to commemorate the sacrifice and celebrate the victory of WWII, yet remains respectful and sensitive to its historic surroundings. The vistas from the Washington Monument to the Lincoln Memorial and the site's park-like settings are preserved, and the double row of elm trees that flank the Memorial have been restored. Above all, the design creates a powerful sense of place that is distinct, memorable, evocative, and serene.

MEMORIAL PLAZA: The plaza and Rainbow Pool are the principal and unifying features of the Memorial. Two poles flying the American flag frame the ceremonial entrance at 17th Street. The bases of granite and bronze are adorned with the military service seals of all the military forces. A series of 24 bronze relief panels along the ceremonial entrance balustrades depict America's war years. Ramps at the north and south approaches provide access to the plaza; granite benches follow the curvilinear rampart walls.

MEMORIAL PAVILIONS: Two 43-foot arched pavilions serve as markers and entries on the north and south ends of the plaza. Within each Pavilion is a "Baldachinos" or "canopy" which is an integral part of the design. Four American eagles hold a suspended victory laurel between their beaks to memorialize

the victory of the WWII generation. Inlaid on the floor of the pavilions is the WWII victory medal surrounded by the years "1941–1945" and the words "Victory on Land," "Victory at Sea," and "Victory in the Air."

PILLARS: Fifty-six granite pillars celebrate the unprecedented unity of the nation during WWII. The pillars are connected by a bronze sculpted rope that symbolizes the bonding of the nation. Each state and territory from that period and the District of Columbia are represented by a pillar adorned with oak and wheat bronze wreaths and inscribed with its name. The 17-foot pillars are open in the center for greater transparency, and ample space between each allows viewing across the Memorial. The states and territories are placed in the order of their entry into the Union beginning at the Freedom Wall and alternating back and forth across the plaza.

COMMEMORATIVE AREA: At the western side of the Memorial, the sacrifice of America's WWII generation and the contribution of our allies is recognized. A field of 4048 sculpted gold stars on the Freedom Wall commemorates the more than 400,000 Americans who gave their lives. During WWII, the gold star was the symbol of family sacrifice.

RAINBOW POOL AND WATERWORKS: The historic waterworks of the Rainbow Pool have been restored and contribute to the celebratory nature of the Memorial. The design provides seating along the pool circumference for visitors. Semi-circular fountains at the base of the two memorial arches and waterfalls flanking the Freedom Wall complement the waterworks in the Rainbow Pool.

LANDSCAPING AND MATERIALS: Two-thirds of the 7.4-acre memorial site is landscaping and water, allowing the memorial to nestle comfortably within its park-like setting. The ceremonial entrance has three large lawn panels between the monumental steps. The double rows of elm trees have been restored and a replanting plan replaced unhealthy trees. A landscaped contemplative area is located at the northwestern corner of the site. Canopies of flowering trees augment the re-seeded lawns.

The Memorial is constructed of bronze and granite. Granite was chosen for its aesthetic appeal, superior strength, durability, and water resistance. The two principal stones selected for the Memorial are "Kershaw" for the vertical elements and "Green County" for the main plaza paving stone. "Kershaw" is quarried in South Carolina, while "Green County" is quarried in Georgia. Two green stones—"Rio Verde" and "Moss Green"—were used for accent paving on the plaza. Both are quarried in Brazil. "Academy Black" and "Mount Airy" were used to reconstruct the Rainbow Pool. "Mount Airy," quarried in North Carolina, is the original coping stone of the Rainbow Pool. To enhance the aesthetic appearance of the water surface of the pool, an apron of "Academy black," quarried in California, was used for the vertical interior spaces.

BAS-RELIEF PANELS: A series of bas-relief sculpture panels created by sculptor Raymond Kaskey were set into the balustrades of the north and south ceremonial entrance walls. The bas-reliefs consist of 24 separate panels. The 12 on the north depict the Atlantic front; the 12 on the south depict the Pacific front.

The unifying theme of the panels is the transformation of America caused by the country's total immersion in World War II. The panels depict the all-out mobilization of America's agricultural, industrial, military, and human resources. This transformed the country into the arsenal of democracy as well as the breadbasket of the world.

The visual inspiration for these panels is the bas-relief sculptures that encircle the Pension Building in Washington, D.C., which were influenced by the bas-reliefs on the Parthenon. What these bas-reliefs have in common is that all are "isocephalic," a Greek word meaning that the heads of the principal figures line up horizontally. The human scale is the unifying element common to all 24 panels. All details, scenes, equipment, etc, are subordinated to the scale of the figure. The unity of purpose unique to this time in America is best evoked by placing the visual emphasis on the individual in this time-honored manner. Most of the panels are based on historical photos.

SCULPTURE:

4 Bronze Columns
8 Bronze Eagles
2 Bronze Laurel Wreaths
24 Bronze Bas Relief Sculptures
4048 Gold Stars
112 Bronze Wreaths with Armatures
52 Bronze Ropes

***Information compiled from fact sheets issued by the American Battle Monuments Commission**

JEWEL OF THE MALL: THE WORLD WAR II MEMORIAL

Design: Jennifer Ehlers
Marketing Design: Jane Howitt and Jessica Warren
Edited: June Brown
Photo Assistance: Jeffery Wilkes and Caitlin Brown
ISBN #978-0-9766150-3-3
Photographs: © Stephen R. Brown 2011
202-667-1965
srb@srbphoto.com

www.wwiimemorialbook.com • www.jewelofthemall.com